...ple
Animals

Melissa Stewart

Enslow Elementary

an imprint of

Enslow Publishers, Inc.
40 Industrial Road
Box 398
Berkeley Heights, NJ 07922
USA
http://www.enslow.com

Enslow Elementary, an imprint of Enslow Publishers, Inc.
Enslow Elementary® is a registered trademark of Enslow Publishers, Inc.

Library of Congress Cataloging-in-Publication Data
Stewart, Melissa.
  Purple animals / Melissa Stewart.
    p. cm. — (All about a rainbow of animals)
  Includes index.
  Summary: "Introduces pre-readers to simple concepts about purple animals using short sentences and
repetition of words"—Provided by publisher.
  ISBN 978-0-7660-4000-7
  1. Animals—Color—Juvenile literature. 2. Purple—Juvenile literature. I. Title.
  QL767.S7438 2012
  590—dc23

                                    2011027407
Future editions:
Paperback ISBN 978-1-4644-0040-7
ePUB ISBN 978-1-4645-0947-6
PDF ISBN 978-1-4645-0947-3

Printed in the United States of America
082014 Bang Printing, Brainerd, Minn.
10 9 8 7 6 5 4 3 2

To Our Readers: We have done our best to make sure all Internet Addresses in this book were active
and appropriate when we went to press. However, the author and the publisher have no control over and
assume no liability for the material available on those Internet sites or on other Web sites they may link
to. Any comments or suggestions can be sent by e-mail to comments@enslow.com or to the address on
the back cover.

Photo Credits: Shutterstock.com: (© Carolyne Pehora, p. 8; © bluehand, pp. 3, 16; © Darren J.
Bradley, p. 12; © Eric Isselee, pp. 3, 6; © Giancarlo Liguori, pp. 1, 10; © Marjan Visser Photography,
p. 14; © Monique Fraters, p. 20; © Tim Balcomb, p. 14; © tntphototravis, p. 21;© Varina and Jay Patel,
p. 4); © Thinkstock, pp. 3, 18 (Jupiterimages).

Cover Photo: Shutterstock.com:©Darren J. Bradley

Note to Parents and Teachers

Help pre-readers get a jumpstart on reading. These lively stories introduce simple concepts with
repetition of words and short simple sentences. Photos and illustrations fill the pages with color and
effectively enhance the text. Free Educator Guides are available for this series at www.enslow.com.
Search for the *All About a Rainbow of Animals* series name.

Contents

Words to Know

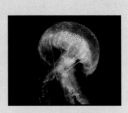

beetle   coral   sea jelly

purple butterfly

purple beetle

purple lizard

purple fish

purple sea star

purple sea slug

purple sea jelly

purple coral

**bird with a
purple head**

purple animals

Read More

Jenkins, Steve. *Living Color.* Boston: Houghton Mifflin, 2007.

Whitehouse, Patricia. *Colors We Eat: Purple and Blue Foods.* Chicago: Heinemann, 2004.

Web Sites

Animal Colors
http://www.highlightskids.com/Science/Stories/SS1000_animalColors.asp

Animal Printable Coloring Pages
http://thecoloringspot.com/animals-coloring-pages/

Index

Guided Reading Level: A
Guided Reading Leveling System is based on the guidelines recommended by Fountas and Pinnell.

Word Count: 26